B55 046 522 7

ROTHERHAM LIBRARY & INFORMATION SERVICE

WIC

17 AUG 2019

12 MAR 2020

KT-558-281

This book must be returned by the date specified at the time of issue as the DUE DATE FOR RETURN
The loan may be extended (personally, by post, telephone or online) for a further period, if the book is not required by another reader, by quoting the barcode / author / title.

Enquiries: 01709 336774

www.rotherham.gov.uk/libraries

Rotherham Libraries	
B55 046 522 7	
PETERS	19-Jun-2019
J791.4372	£7.99
	WIC

DISNEY · PIXAR

TOY STORY 4

THE OFFICIAL GUIDE

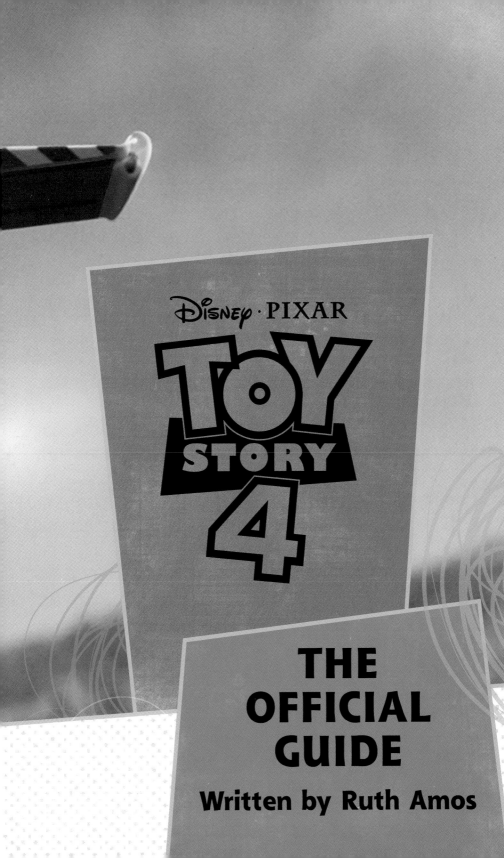

Disney · PIXAR

TOY STORY 4

THE OFFICIAL GUIDE

Written by Ruth Amos

Contents

Introduction

The toys are back in town! Woody, Buzz and the gang are getting used to life with their new owner, Bonnie. But adventure lies just around the corner as the gang sets off on a road trip and a clueless new toy causes chaos! Will everybody make it back in one piece?

Woody

Faithful friend

Cowboy doll Woody is the most loyal toy that any kid could wish for. This kind, lovable sheriff and his gang of toy friends are getting used to life with their new owner, Bonnie.

Things you need to know about Woody

1 Woody is a vintage toy, made in the late 1950s.

2 He has a voice box sewn inside him with a pull cord.

3 Sometimes he cares a bit too much about his kid owner and doesn't realise there is more to life.

4 Woody's old owner, Andy, gifted all his toys to Bonnie when he grew up.

9

Facing the future

Life isn't always easy for Woody in Bonnie's room. She already has her own set of toys, and Woody is a new toy on the block. Sometimes he misses the old days with Andy.

Blast from the past

Woody is shocked to spot a bedside lamp in a shop window. His old friend Bo Peep was part of the lamp, which once belonged to Andy's sister, Molly. Woody hasn't seen Bo since Molly gave her and the lamp away, years ago.

Hat can be thrown like a boomerang at targets

Did you know?
Woody can use his pull string like a lasso to catch people!

Hard-working cowboy
When Bonnie's new toy needs rescuing, Woody considers it his duty to bring him back to Bonnie – whatever the cost. Once Woody has made his mind up, he can be a bit stubborn!

Cowboy riding boots with golden spurs

Who's who?

Meet the gang! Lots of different toys live in Bonnie's bedroom. Cuddly and plastic, alien and animal – toys of all shapes and sizes can be found here!

Woody

Jessie

Bullseye

Hamm

Mr. Pricklepants

Slinky Dog

12

Trixie

Rex

Buzz

Buttercup

Dolly

Alien

Mrs. Potato Head

Mr. Potato Head

Forky

Bonnie

Creative kid

Five-year-old Bonnie is a bright, kind child with a big imagination! She loves to play with her toys, invent new games and go on make-believe adventures.

Things you need to know about Bonnie

1 She likes to build a makeshift town and play with her toys in it.

2 Bonnie goes on a road trip with her family, and she's very excited.

3 She is really sad when she loses her new toy, Forky.

4 Bonnie loves to play on the swing with her toys.

Growing up

Bonnie has to start kindergarten, and she is not very happy about it. She would much rather be playing a game with her toys at home!

Stowaway sheriff

Bonnie wants to take a toy with her to kindergarten on her first day, but she's not allowed to. Bonnie doesn't know that Woody sneaks into her rucksack to keep an eye on her!

Purple rucksack often gets left behind by Bonnie

Did you know?
Bonnie loves drawing, colouring in and making things.

Old-time toys
Kind-hearted Bonnie looks after all her toys well. Some of the older toys from her toddler days get left in the cupboard nowadays, but they understand it's all just part of her growing up.

Stripy leggings are great for running and climbing

Children chat to each other in excitement

Kindergarten

Kindergarten seems like a fun place. There are lots of activities to do, interesting things to learn and new friends to meet – but poor Bonnie is finding it all a bit scary!

Bright pictures and a map cover the walls

Bonnie looks around the room shyly

19

Woody to the rescue

It's craft time at kindergarten, but Bonnie is upset when another kid takes away her art supplies. Luckily, Woody has a plan!

1 Scan the room – the art supplies are being thrown away into a rubbish bin.

2 Check that the coast is clear before you leave your hiding spot.

3 Carefully climb down from the cubbyholes to the floor.

4 Use a lunch box as cover while running over to the rubbish bin.

5 Leap inside and hunt for different objects that Bonnie can use.

6 Keep a sharp eye out for passing teachers and children.

7 Wait until Bonnie is distracted, and then leave the supplies on her desk. Mission accomplished!

Making Forky

Bonnie puts her brilliant imagination to the test. She uses the random objects that Woody found in the rubbish bin to build something new – a brand new friend called Forky!

Red pipe cleaner for arms

A spork for the body and face

Sticky tack glues body to feet

Ice lolly stick broken in half for feet

Googly eyes

Feet marked with Bonnie's name in felt-tip pen

23

Forky

Confused new toy

After Bonnie makes Forky, he is like a baby – he has to learn how to walk and talk. But all this scared spork wants is to climb into the nearest rubbish bin, where he feels warm, cosy and safe.

Things you need to know about Forky

1 Forky is scared of Bonnie at first because she's so much bigger.

2 As a spork, Forky says he was made for eating soup, salad and chilli.

3 Woody has to babysit Forky constantly since he keeps trying to climb into the rubbish.

4 Later, he wants to be with Bonnie, because he believes he is her rubbish!

Bonnie's room

Bright and cosy, Bonnie's colourful room is full of fun, just like its owner. The squishy bed is perfect for jumping on. Baskets and boxes are filled with toys and games, ready for playtime!

Mobile with stars and rainbows hangs over bed

Box full of dressing-up accessories

Homemade cardboard spaceship

Buzz Lightyear

Brave space ranger

Awesome space explorer Buzz is always ready for a new challenge. Buzzing with energy, he loves to team up with sidekick Woody. To infinity and beyond!

Things you need to know about Buzz Lightyear

1 Buzz is Woody's best friend.

2 When Woody doesn't return from a mission to bring back Forky, Buzz sets off to find him.

3 Buzz thinks the voice that plays when he presses his spacesuit buttons must belong to his conscience!

4 He gets pinned up as a prize at a fairground by accident.

Dolly

Born leader

Rag doll Dolly takes charge of the toys in Bonnie's room and makes sure everything runs smoothly. She is great at keeping calm in a crisis!

Things you need to know about Dolly

1 Dolly plays the part of the mayor in Bonnie's pretend town game.

2 She welcomes any new toys and makes sure they are happy.

3 Dolly warns all the toys whenever Bonnie is about to enter a room so they can freeze in toy mode.

4 She thinks Woody can be a little bit dramatic sometimes.

Bonnie's parents

Caring mum and dad

Bonnie's parents are really proud of their little girl. They know she is scared to start kindergarten, but they are sure that she will have fun there.

Things you need to know about Bonnie's parents

1 They try to reassure Bonnie that kindergarten will be fine.

2 As a reward for being brave, they surprise Bonnie with a road trip holiday!

3 They spend a long time hunting for Bonnie's missing new toy, Forky.

4 They cheer her up when she's upset.

Road trip

Adventure time! Bonnie and her parents set off on holiday in their camper van. There is plenty of space inside for Forky, Woody and the rest of the toy gang.

TriCounty RV
CALL TO RENT!

Comfy ride
The big camper van has comfy beds for tired travellers. It also has a pull-out canopy so the family can relax in the shade.

Artist at work

The dining table is a good spot for Bonnie to draw. Her toys are lined up alongside, ready for playtime.

Did you know?
The family makes a stop at the old-fashioned town of Grand Basin.

Great escapes?

Forky keeps trying to escape from Bonnie and leap into the nearest rubbish bin. Exhausted Woody always brings him back, but this confused utensil just tries again!

Hiding on the flower on Bonnie's rucksack when she goes outside

"Freedom!"

Launching himself towards the rubbish bin on the camper van

Jumping out of the camper van window

TRiCOUNTY
CALL TO RENT!

How to be a good toy

Forky knows nothing about being a toy – he doesn't even understand what a toy is! It's up to patient Woody to explain the rules.

Always be there for Bonnie and look out for her when she is scared or sad.

Stay in **toy mode** whenever Bonnie or her family are in the room.

Be ready at all times for Bonnie to play with you.

"You have to be there for Bonnie. That is your job."

Help Bonnie create **happy childhood memories** that she will remember all her life.

Watch over Bonnie as she grows up and becomes an adult.

If you get lost, you should **make your way back to Bonnie** as soon as possible!

Combat Carl Jr. action figures lie in the sandpit

Kids play games with lost toys they've found

The playground

Watch out! The playground is always full of children, ready to play with any toys they might find here. For lost toys like Bo Peep, it's super exciting when a new group of kids arrive here – but Woody would much prefer to be with his owner!

Woody is launched on baby swing high into air

Bonnie's name written on sole of Woody's boot

41

Bo Peep

Confident adventurer

Shepherdess Bo Peep has spent years as a lost toy with no owner. She travels between playgrounds, plays with different children and then moves on. Bo loves the freedom and excitement that it brings her!

Things you need to know about Bo Peep

1 Andy's family gave Bo away. She was later sold to an antiques shop, which she decided to leave.

2 She is made of porcelain, a fragile ceramic material.

3 Bo often gets chipped or broken by kids, but she doesn't mind. She just glues herself back together!

4 She bumps into Woody in the playground. Surprise!

43

A lost toy

Woody is horrified to discover that Bo is now a lost toy, with no owner. But Bo wouldn't swap her life for anything! She is independent, and she is following her dreams.

Long, hooked staff is light but strong

Star support

Woody is in awe of Bo's ability to champion other toys and make them believe in themselves. It will be crucial for their upcoming mission!

44

Broken arm
mended
with tape

Skirt
turned into
cool cape

Tactical expert

Bo agrees to help Woody
rescue Forky from the
antiques shop. She is great
at planning risky missions,
and she knows the place
well. Bo also has some
special toy contacts who
might be able to help!

Did you know?

Bo has been a lost
toy for seven years.
She has seen so many
fantastic things
during that time!

Cool moves

Bo Peep is on the move! She can leap, climb and sprint, but it's not just her feet that are fast – her expert handiwork turns her staff into a multipurpose tool.

Speedy Bo is great at dodging kids' trampling feet and weaving in and out of obstacles.

Bo isn't afraid of heights and always lands on her feet after a big fall.

The staff makes a good weapon for whacking enemies or tripping them up.

46

Bo can hold out her staff to pull a climbing toy up to a high spot.

Bo can even use her hook to slide down a zip wire or clear away cobwebs!

Bo uses her long staff in a rescue operation to help reach a toy in danger.

Operation Pull-Toy

Years ago, Woody and Bo Peep once pulled off an amazing rescue mission! The pair worked together with Andy's other toys to save RC the car. Talk about teamwork!

1 Locate the victim

Spotted! RC is stranded outside the house in a raging storm!

2 Create a launch pad

Bo builds a launch pad with a book and an armadillo toy. Jessie gets on it.

Open the window

Jessie is launched up to the sill and opens the window.

3

Lower Woody down

4 Woody climbs on Slinky Dog and abseils down the side of the house as the others hold Slinky's feet.

5 ## Disaster!

Slinky has run out of stretch! Woody can't reach RC.

Plan B

6 Bo attaches a long line of toy monkeys to her hook and adds it to Slinky's spring.

Heave!

7 Woody lunges forwards and grabs RC. The toys pull them back up to the window. RC is safe!

49

Billy, Goat and Gruff

Bo Peep's faithful flock

This trio of porcelain sheep love their fun lives as lost toys. Attached together in one big fleece, they follow Bo loyally wherever her adventures take them.

Things you need to know about Billy, Goat and Gruff

1 The sheep help Bo collect random objects to use for repairs in case they get damaged.

2 They used to be part of Molly's bedside lamp, along with Bo.

3 They love winning races.

4 They're not impressed when Woody forgets their names and thinks they are boys.

Giggle McDimples

Tiny detective

Officer Giggle McDimples runs the Pet Patrol, searching the streets for missing pets. Clever and funny, Giggle is Bo's best friend and travel buddy.

Things you need to know about Giggle McDimples

1 Giggle is half an inch tall.

2 She searches for pets such as ants, caterpillars and miniature poodles.

3 Giggle sits on Bo's shoulder to speak to her.

4 She can fit inside the keyhole of a door, spin around like a lockpick and unlock it!

Wall map shows last sightings of missing pets

Pet Patrol deputy joins Giggle in her office for meeting

Patrol car parked outside on drive

54

PET PATROL

Giggle McDimples

Perfectly portable
The Pet Patrol is shaped like a police officer's badge. When Giggle and Bo are travelling to a new place, it fits neatly inside Bo's skunkmobile vehicle.

Pet Patrol headquarters

When she isn't patrolling Mini-opolis city for missing animals, Giggle works at the Pet Patrol headquarters. This tiny office has everything she needs to organise her next search and rescue mission.

Tail is made from feather duster

Roomy ride
There's plenty of space inside the vehicle for Bo, the three sheep, Giggle and Woody during their adventures!

Furry material hides the car's wheels

56

Skunkmobile

Bo Peep built this skunklike vehicle using a motorised toy car and objects found on her travels. It's a good way to get around quickly – most people leap out of the way when they see a scary skunk on the prowl!

Did you know?
Billy, Goat and Gruff drive the vehicle. They aren't great drivers – they nearly run over poor Woody by accident.

Nose is made from old bottle cap

Combat Carl Jrs.

Non-stop action figures

The cool Combat Carl Jr. soldiers are based in the playground. These lost toys don't just wait around for children to find them – they always keep a lookout for the next good playtime opportunity!

Things you need to know about the Combat Carl Jrs.

1 The Combat Carls like to run everywhere in a group, chanting "Hut. Hut. Hut." as they go.

2 Their names are Combat Carl, Ice Attack Combat Carl and Volcano Attack Combat Carl.

3 They're very impressed to discover Woody has an owner.

4 They love to gatecrash big birthday parties – it means there will be plenty of kids to play with them!

Who is your perfect sidekick?

Adventures can be a risky business, so you need the perfect toy partner by your side. Who would be your accomplice?

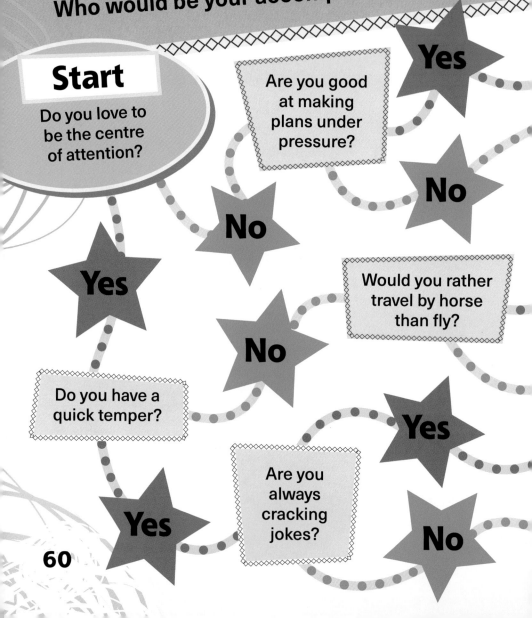

Start

Do you love to be the centre of attention?

Are you good at making plans under pressure?

Yes

No

No

Yes

Would you rather travel by horse than fly?

No

Do you have a quick temper?

Yes

Are you always cracking jokes?

Yes

No

60

Is money important to you?

Yes

Hamm

No

Giggle McDimples

Are you great at acting?

Yes

Trixie

No

Yes

No

Jessie

Rex

Mr. Potato Head

Mr. Pricklepants

Buzz Lightyear

Antiques shop

From old furniture and signs to unusual trinkets and treasures, the Second Chance Antiques shop is full of surprises. Customers never know what they might find here!

Vintage gumball machines

Teatime

The shop owner's granddaughter, Harmony, uses an old china set and a little stool for pretend tea parties.

Margaret, the shop owner, chats to her daughter, Carol

Cabinet filled with valuable jewellery and knick-knacks

63

Gabby Gabby

Lonely doll

Vintage doll Gabby Gabby lives in a cabinet in the antiques shop. She spends the long days dreaming of a happy future with a child owner who loves her. If only she weren't broken!

Things you need to know about Gabby Gabby

1 Since her voice box is broken, kids don't play with her.

2 Gabby Gabby loves tea parties and practises holding her cup correctly.

3 Her antique pram is her preferred mode of transport.

4 She has a gang of dummies in the shop who do everything she says.

Bright future?

Gabby Gabby is delighted when she meets Woody and Forky in the shop. She notices Woody's voice box right away and wants to learn all about him. Perhaps he can help her?

Stop that fork!
Gabby Gabby orders her dummies to capture Forky and Woody when they get scared and try to leave. They manage to catch Forky, but Woody escapes!

66

Red hair
worn in
bunches

A chance
to be loved

Gabby Gabby keeps Forky
in the shop, because she
knows Woody will come back
for him. But she treats Forky
kindly – she just wants to talk
to Woody and plead for her
own opportunity to have a kid.

Neat, yellow
polka-dot
dress

Did you
know?

Gabby Gabby loves
to read her own
storybook, *Gabby
Gabby: A Very
Special Day.*

Benson

Creepy henchman

Ventriloquist's dummy Benson is Gabby Gabby's chief sidekick. This smartly dressed menace leads a gang of dummies and is always on the lookout for trouble.

Things you need to know about Benson

1 He guards Gabby Gabby's cabinet and pushes her around in her pram.

2 He wears a pinstripe suit and a red bow tie.

3 Benson captures Forky under Gabby Gabby's orders.

4 There are three scary dummies in Benson's team.

Giant Ferris wheel has amazing views

Aeroplanes dip and spin around on ride

70

The carnival

The travelling carnival has come to Grand Basin! This fun-filled fairground is bursting with scary rides, whirling carousels and exciting game booths.

Brightly coloured game and food stalls

Customers queue to go on ride

"If you think you can just show up and take our top prize spot, you're wrong."
Bunny

Ducky and Bunny

Bickering buddies

Cuddly toys Ducky and Bunny have spent years as fairground prizes, waiting to be won by a child. This scrappy pair has a lot of arguments!

Things you need to know about Ducky and Bunny

1 Ducky and Bunny are attached together by the hand.

2 They have been prizes at the Star Adventurer booth for three years.

3 When Buzz arrives as a prize, they think he's trying to cheat and be won by a kid first!

4 They end up joining Buzz on the mission to find Forky.

Big squabbles!

Bunny and Ducky always seem to be arguing about something. Perhaps it's because they have to spend so much time together – all day, every day!

What do you mean? Bunny gets cross when Ducky doesn't explain things properly. After all, Bunny isn't a mind reader!

Help! Ducky can't believe he actually has to point out how short his legs are to get Bunny's help to kick Buzz!

Me, me, me! In a deal, Woody promises to take Bunny and Ducky to meet Bonnie. But which cute animal will she love more? The argument rages on.

Hurry up! When Buzz escapes the booth, the pair chase after him. Ducky is irritated when Bunny gets stuck – giving Buzz a big head start!

Pardon? Ducky says Bunny needs to work on paying attention and his listening skills.

Duke Caboom

Cool stunt toy

Famous Canadian motorbike star Duke Caboom may be a show-off, but he doesn't really believe in himself. After he was rejected by his kid owner, poor Duke lost all his confidence.

Things you need to know about Duke Caboom

1. Duke hangs out with other toys inside the pinball machine at the antiques shop.

2. Duke's kid, Rejean, threw Duke away when he couldn't land a big motorbike jump and crashed.

3. He has a handlebar moustache and wears a maple leaf–patterned cape.

4. Duke tries to help Bo, Woody and their team rescue Forky.

78

Stunt motorbike

Duke Caboom is never seen without his vintage motorbike. It might be a bit battered these days, but it can still take him on an epic ride!

Did you know?

Duke rides down the antiques shop aisle, making Dragon the shop cat chase after him. This distracts Dragon away from the other toys!

Tyre worn from Duke's crashes

Powerful launcher

Duke's toy set includes a launcher. Pushing down the handle launches the motorbike into the air for big jumps.

DUKE CABOOM

Maple leaf symbol

Big silver engine

Daredevil poses

Duke Caboom loves to put on a show with his mighty motorbike moves. He's Canada's greatest stuntman!

1 Crouching up on the seat

Leaping over the handlebars **2**

3 Pretending to fly

4 Standing on the seat, hands on hips

5 Leaning back with legs in the air

"What do we DO?!"

Mrs. Potato Head

Jessie

Quick-thinking cowgirl

Cheerful Jessie is really clever. She is full of bright ideas to prevent Bonnie's family from leaving town before Woody has returned from his mission!

Things you need to know about Jessie

1 She greets Forky with her typical "Howdy!" when they first meet.

2 Jessie plays the part of the sheriff in Bonnie's town game.

3 She thinks of a great idea to make Bonnie's dad drive to the carnival, by getting Trixie to mimic the voice of the satnav. Turn right!

4 Jessie sneaks into Bonnie's rucksack to keep an eye on her when she starts school.

Operation Flat Tyre

Yikes! Bonnie's mum and dad are about to drive off – but Buzz and Woody are still not back from their mission to save Forky! What's a cowgirl to do?

1

Stay focused

Jessie focuses on the problem as the other toys argue and panic. She has a brilliant idea. Light bulb moment!

Bad ideas...
Buttercup suggests the toys frame Dad for a crime so he gets put in prison. Rex suggests they go back in time to warn Woody about the future!

2

Travel to the target

Jessie jumps out of the camper van's window and sneaks up to one of the front tyres.

3 Identify target and attack

Jessie punctures the tyre with a sharp nail. The air escapes, and the tyre goes flat.

4 Return to safety

She returns to the back of the vehicle and climbs back through the window.

5 Enjoy the adoring crowd

The rest of the toys are amazed by her daring mission!

Living like Bo

Over the years, Bo has travelled far and wide, meeting different children and discovering new places. She has learnt so much along the way!

DO live in the moment, and say yes to fun.
Piñata party? Why not?!

DO be prepared.
Bo collects repair supplies during her travels in case she gets broken during playtime.

DO make your own happiness.
Bo appreciates the small things in life, like a beautiful view.

DO be confident in your abilities.
Bo knows exactly which child will be a good match to play with a toy.

DO help others to see the best in themselves.
Bo encourages other toys to use their strengths.

DON'T rely on one kid to make you happy.
There are so many different kids out there with different interests.

DON'T waste time waiting for things to happen.
Bo and Giggle spent years on the shelf in the antiques shop, waiting to be bought.

DON'T be afraid to try new things.
Bo travels from place to place and enjoys seeing new parts of the world.

DON'T always put others first, no matter the cost.
Bo knows it's important to look after herself as well as her friends.

Which toy are you?

Discover which awesome toy you are most like! Is it Duke Caboom, Bo Peep or Woody?

1 **How would you describe your personality?**
A   A show-off
B   Adventurous
C   Loyal

2 **You must take a risk to help a friend, but it's scary. Do you?**
A   Try to avoid the situation – but if you can't, then just hope for the best.
B   Take your time – check out the situation, use your experience and be confident.
C   Go for it – your friend needs you right now, and there's no time to lose.

3 **Pick an accessory!**
A   A helmet
B   A cape
C   A cowboy hat

4

What are your favourite hobbies?

A Acting and singing
B Exploring and building things
C Playing and being with friends

5

What do you find trickiest?

A Believing in yourself
B Admitting when you feel hurt
C Listening to others when you disagree with them

Mostly As – Duke Caboom
You love to be the star of the show and make people laugh. You're brave, but you don't always believe in yourself.

Mostly Bs – Bo Peep
You're a real adventurer and love trying new things. You're clever and know how to bring out the best in people.

Mostly Cs – Woody
You're really kind and would do anything for your friends. You never give up and always try your hardest.

94

"You have this way of making a toy see the best in themselves."
Woody

Penguin
Random
House

Senior Editor Ruth Amos
Senior Designer Lynne Moulding
Pre-production Producer Siu Yin Chan
Senior Producer Jonathan Wakeham
Managing Editor Sadie Smith
Managing Art Editor Vicky Short
Publisher Julie Ferris
Art Director Lisa Lanzarini
Publishing Director Simon Beecroft

First published in Great Britain in 2019 by
Dorling Kindersley Limited
80 Strand, London WC2R 0RL
A Penguin Random House Company

10 9 8 7 6 5 4 3 2 1
001–311502–May/2019

Page design copyright © 2019 Dorling Kindersley Limited

Copyright © 2019 Disney Enterprises, Inc. and Pixar.
All rights reserved.

© POOF-Slinky, LLC.

BARREL OF MONKEYS, MR. POTATO HEAD, and MRS. POTATO
HEAD are trademarks of Hasbro and used with permission.
© Hasbro. All rights reserved.

All rights reserved. Without limiting the rights under
the copyright reserved above, no part of this publication
may be reproduced, stored in, or introduced into a
retrieval system, or transmitted, in any form, or by any
means (electronic, mechanical, photocopying, recording,
or otherwise), without the prior written permission
of the copyright owner.

A CIP catalogue record for this book
is available from the British Library.

ISBN: 978-0-24135-756-9

Printed in Slovakia

A WORLD OF IDEAS:
SEE ALL THERE IS TO KNOW

www.dk.com
www.disney.com